WEIGHT LOSS RECIPES

-no sugar, no flour, made deliciously easy-

COOKBOOK

Whole Food, Plant Based, & Vegan Volume

Books by Natalie Aul

1. Weight Loss Recipes Cookbook **Volume 1**
2. Weight Loss Recipes Cookbook **Volume 2**
3. Weight Loss Recipes Cookbook **Volume 3**
4. Weight Loss Recipes Cookbook **Volume 4**
5. Weight Loss Recipes Cookbook **Volume 5**
6. Weight Loss Recipes Cookbook **Volume 6**
7. Weight Loss Recipes Cookbook **Volume 7**
8. Cooking with Joy
9. Weight Loss Recipes Cookbook **Whole Food, Plant Based, & Vegan Volume**
10. Simply Delicious **A 14 Day Food Plan**

Copyright © 2020 by Natalie Aul

All rights reserved. No part of this publication may be reproduced, stored in a retrieval system, or transmitted by any means – electronic, mechanical, photocopying, recording, or otherwise – without prior written permission from the author. The only exception is for the furtherance of the Gospel of salvation, or brief quotations in printed reviews.

Scripture quotations are from the King James Version of the Bible if not otherwise indicated.

Scripture quotations marked TPT are from The Passion Translation®. Copyright © 2017, 2018 by Passion & Fire Ministries, Inc. Used by permission. All rights reserved. ThePassionTranslation.com. All Scripture quotations are from The Passion Translation®. Copyright © 2017, 2018 by Passion & Fire Ministries, Inc. Used by permission. All rights reserved. ThePassionTranslation.com.

"Scripture quotations taken from the Amplified® Bible (AMP), Copyright © 2015 by The Lockman Foundation
Used by permission. www.Lockman.org"

"Scripture quotations taken from the Amplified® Bible (AMPC), Copyright © 1954, 1958, 1962, 1964, 1965, 1987 by The Lockman Foundation Used by permission. www.Lockman.org"

Scripture taken from The Message. Copyright © 1993, 1994, 1995, 1996, 2000, 2001, 2002. Used by permission of NavPress Publishing Group.

Printed in the United States of America

"Blessed are the pure in heart for they shall see God."
Matthew 5:8

Purebooks artwork by Jessica Benson

Special Thanks to:

My sister Kelly, without you this book would not be possible!

My mom Maggie, for your encouragement, and introducing us to this new way of life.

To everyone who has sent me encouraging notes and such lovely reviews of my other cookbook volumes, you have all been so sweet!

I give all the glory to God, without Him I can do nothing.

Contents

Breakfast

<u>Page</u>

12 Peanut Butter Jelly Oatmeal

14 PB&J Breakfast Cookies

16 Peanut Butter Granola

18 Banana Oatmeal Cookies

20 Peanut Butter Apple Cinnamon Oatmeal

22 Blueberry Chickpea Breakfast Blondies

24 Banana Nut Oatmeal

26 Apple Rhubarb Jam Waffles

28 Pumpkin Blondies

30 Banana Apple Nut Pops

32 PB&J Muffins

34 Sweet Potato Pie

36 Apple Walnut Bars

38 Raw-nola

40 Hot Pink Granola

42 Apple Granola

44 Peanut Butter Banana Granola Bars

46 Peanut Butter Toasty Granola

48 Sweet Potato Black Bean Burger

Lunch

56 Cinnamon Banana Chickpea Bombs

58 Chickpea Cookie Dough

60 Chickpea Blondies

62 Chickpea Cookies

64 Key lime Chia Drops

66 Apple Chickpea Cinnamon Rolls

68 Chickpea Banana Cinnamon Rolls

70 Chickpea Cinnamon Rolls

72 Chickpea Fruit Pies

74 Carrot Spice Slaw

76 Apple Pie with Peanut Butter Chickpea Crust

78 Mini Pies

80 Peanut butter Chia Bites

82 Sesame Protein Balls
84 Hot Pink Beet Hummus
86 Coconut Protein Balls
88 Red Beet Slaw with Rosemary Tahini Dressing
90 Ginger Chickpea Asian Salad
92 B&B Blondie Bars
94 Coconut Tahini Flax Bites
96 Coconut Tahini Soft Serve

Dinner

102 Slow Cooker Veggie Sloppy Joe
104 Cabbage Egg Rolls
106 Crockpot Fajita Vegetables

Sauces, Seasonings, and Sides

110 Seed Crackers
112 Apple Banana Rhubarb Chia Jelly
114 Strawberry Rhubarb Jam

116 Tahini Ranch Dressing

118 Cauliflower Stuffing

120 Squashed Brussel Sprouts Carrots and Spinach Stir Fry

122 Easy Guacamole

124 Roasted Nuts

126 Toasted Sesame Seeds

128 Apple Chia Jam

130 Southwest Black Bean Hummus

132 Jicama Tortillas

134 Cranberry Sauce

136 Cinnamon Roasted Squash Seeds

138 Rosemary Tahini Dressing

140 Aquafaba

142 Bubble Tea

144 Cranberry Apple Chia Jam

146 Taco Seasoning

Food addiction is not like other addictions. Most addictions you can stop cold turkey but you can't exactly do that with food. Most diets fail, are not realistic, or sustainable. "Run 20 miles, do 30 burpee's, then hike Mount Everest. You will be skinny in no time!" or "Eat our pre-made food… it tastes like card board and you will be starving most of the time." Or "Eat only baked fish and broccoli." or "Take these pills, and drink this potion and BAM thin!" These yo-yo diets don't deal with the real problem and you can't live on pills or climb Mount Everest forever… so the weight comes back.

What if I told you there was a better way to lose weight, be healthy, and keep the weight off? You even get to eat a lot of delicious food without starving! If I can do it, a chunky kid who loved pizza, ice cream, and mac & cheese, you can do it! I will do the hard part and give you all the recipes.

What's the plan?

Sugar free, flour free, 3 weighed meals a day (no snacks in between). In addition, you will be Happy, Healthy, Skinny, and FREE!

Natalie

Breakfast

Breakfast = 1 protein, 1 fruit (6oz), and 1 grain.

PB&J for breakfast? Oh yeah!

Peanut Butter Jelly Oatmeal

Ingredients:

1oz Uncooked oats (full grain)

1/2oz Chia seeds (1/4 protein)

1/2oz Slivered almonds (1/4 protein)

6oz total: Frozen Blueberries and Strawberries (full fruit)

6oz Water

1oz Peanut butter (1/2 protein)

Directions: In a microwave safe bowl, add uncooked oats, chia seeds, almonds, blueberries, strawberries, and water. Microwave for 2 min. In a separate bowl add peanut butter and 1Tbsp hot water, stir until smooth (repeat until desired consistency) drizzle peanut butter over oatmeal.

Super quick and easy. Perfect for traveling!

PB&J Breakfast Cookies

Ingredients:

1oz Uncooked oats (full grain)

1oz Peanut butter (1/2 protein)

1oz Walnuts (Almonds or whatever nut you want) (1/2 protein)

6oz total: Banana, and Mixed berries. (Strawberries and Blueberries) (full fruit)

Pinch of each: Sea salt, cinnamon

Directions: Preheat oven to 375. Mix all ingredients together. Drop onto a parchment paper lined baking sheet (spread out your cookies for a crispier cookie or leave them in cookie size balls for a doughy cookie) bake for 18 min. or microwave for 4 min.

Super yummy on top of 4oz plain Greek yogurt with 6oz strawberries and bananas.

Peanut Butter Granola

Ingredients:

4oz Uncooked oats

2oz Nuts (Almonds, flax seeds, chia seeds, hemp seeds, and walnuts, or any nuts you desire)

2oz Peanut butter

Directions: Preheat oven to 300°. Mix uncooked oats, nuts, and peanut butter. Spread mix onto a pan lined with parchment paper (you can use a nonstick pan instead.) Bake in oven 15-20min until golden brown or the darkness you want. Stir every 3-5min so it does not burn. Once cooked immediately place on plate and refrigerate to make it crispy. Once cooled split into 4 baggies.

1 baggie = 1/2 protein, and 1 grain serving.

Side with ½ protein and 6oz fruit for a complete breakfast

Perfect for travel. Make the day of, or the night before and chill in the fridge. Surprisingly filling!

Banana Oatmeal Cookies

Ingredients:

6oz Banana (full fruit)

1oz Peanut butter (1/2 protein)

1oz Uncooked oatmeal (full grain)

1oz total: Ground Flax seeds, chia seeds, slivered almonds (1/2 protein)

Pinch of each: Sea salt, cinnamon, vanilla extract

Directions: Mix all ingredients together. Divide and make 4 cookies on a plate, sprinkle more cinnamon on top and microwave 3-4 min. serve hot, sprinkle with sea salt, or refrigerate overnight

DO NOT MIX THIS AFTER ITS COOKED! It will destroy the delicious caramelyness.

Peanut Butter Apple Cinnamon Oatmeal

Ingredients:

1oz Uncooked oatmeal (full grain)

6oz Apple (full fruit)

Cinnamon

4-5oz Water

1oz Peanut butter (1/2 protein)

Directions: In a bowl, add oatmeal, chopped apple, cinnamon, and water. Mix and top with more cinnamon, microwave for 2 minutes. In separate bowl, add peanut butter and 1Tbsp hot water and mix until smooth (repeat until peanut butter is drizzly). Drizzle peanut butter over top of your oatmeal.

Side with ½ protein for a complete breakfast

Blueberry Chickpea Breakfast Blondies

Ingredients:

3oz Canned chickpeas (1/2 protein)

1oz Peanut butter (1/2 protein)

4oz Banana (2/3 fruit)

2oz Frozen blueberries (1/3 fruit)

1oz Uncooked oats (full grain)

Pinch of each: Baking powder, baking soda, sea salt, vanilla extract

Directions: Preheat oven to 350°. Add all ingredients in a food processor (except frozen blueberries and oats) mix until smooth. (or blend chickpeas, peanut butter, and seasonings until smooth, then add banana and mash.). Stir in frozen blueberries, and uncooked oats. Pour mixture into an oiled oven safe baking dish and Bake for 25-30min. Sprinkle with course sea salt.

Sweet and salty a perfect combination!

Banana Nut Oatmeal

Ingredients:

1oz Uncooked oats (full grain)

1/2oz Chia seeds (1/4 protein)

Pinch of each: Sea salt, cinnamon

6oz Banana (full fruit)

6oz Water

1oz Whole oven roasted and salted almonds (1/2 protein)

1/2oz Peanut butter (1/4 protein)

Directions: Chop banana. Add uncooked oats, chia seeds, salt, cinnamon, ½ of banana, and water. Microwave for 2 min. Top with almonds, peanut butter and remaining chopped banana, mix and enjoy.

Apple Rhubarb Jam Waffles

Ingredients:

1oz Uncooked oats (full grain)

4oz Apple rhubarb jam* (2/3 fruit)

3oz Chickpeas (1/2 protein)

Pinch of each: Baking powder, sea salt

1/4tsp Cinnamon

Directions: Mash/blend all ingredients together. Pour batter into a waffle maker. Top with fruit and protein.

Side with 2oz fruit, and ½ protein for a complete breakfast.

Find apple rhubarb jam in "Sauces, Seasonings, and Sides"

Delicious hot or cold

Pumpkin Blondies

Ingredients:

1oz Peanut butter (1/2 protein)

1oz Uncooked oats (full grain)

3oz Chickpeas (1/2 protein)

3oz Banana (1/2 fruit)

3oz Pumpkin (1/2 fruit)

Pinch of each: Baking powder, sea salt, vanilla extract

Pumpkin pie spice: 1/4tsp Ginger, 1/4tsp nutmeg, 1/2tsp cinnamon, 1/8tsp clove

Directions: Preheat oven to 350. Blend/mash chickpeas. Add rest of ingredients and mix well. Scoop mixture into small baking dish and bake 30min. Let cool 10 min before eating.

Perfect for on the go!

Banana Apple Nut Pops

Ingredients:

1oz Uncooked oats (full grain)

6oz total: Banana, apple jam* (full fruit)

1/2oz Walnuts (1/4 protein)

2oz Plain Greek yogurt (1/4 protein)

1oz Peanut butter (1/2 protein)

Directions: Mix and mash all ingredients together. Scoop mixture into Popsicle molds (or line a Tupperware with plastic wrap and scoop in mixture to make a bar) Place in freezer 3-4hours of overnight.

*Find Apple Jam in Sauces, Sides, and Seasonings

Deliciously gooey!

PB&J Muffins

Ingredients:

1oz Uncooked oats (full grain)

6oz total: Strawberry, banana

1/2oz Ground flax seeds (1/4 protein)

1 1/2oz Warm water

1oz Peanut butter (1/2 protein)

Pinch of each: Baking powder, baking soda, vanilla extract

1/2oz Peanut butter (1/4 protein)

Directions: Preheat oven to 350. Mix ground flax seed, water, and let sit 5-10min to form a gel. Mix oats, fruit, 1oz peanut butter spices and flax gel. Pour mixture into muffin tins. In a separate bowl, mix peanut butter and a slash of hot water, stir until smooth, repeat until drizzly consistency. Drizzle peanut butter over muffins and bake 25-30min until a toothpick comes out clean

The peanut butter chickpea crust is amazing and the sea salt adds the perfect amount of sweet and salty!

Sweet Potato Pie

Ingredients:

3oz Chickpeas (1/2 protein)

1/2oz Peanut butter (1/4 protein)

Pinch of each: Baking soda, baking salt, sea salt, maple extract

4oz Cooked sweet potato (full grain)

2oz Milk (1/4 protein)

2oz Banana (1/3 fruit)

1tsp Pumpkin pie spice

Directions: Preheat oven to 375. Blend/mix chickpeas, peanut butter, baking soda, baking powder, and sea salt. Split dough into 2 parts, place dough between 2 wax papers and roll thin. In a separate bowl mix sweet potato, maple extract, milk, banana, and pumpkin pie spice. Place half of dough in a lightly oiled pie tin, pour sweet potato mixture onto dough, and place other half of dough on top. Use a fork to press the edge of dough together, score an X on the top of the pie and bake 20-30min.

Side with 4oz fruit for a complete breakfast

Apple Walnut Bars

Ingredients:

4oz Apple (2/3 fruit)

1oz Uncooked oats (full grain)

1 1/4oz Walnuts (1/2+1/8 protein)

1/4oz Ground flax seeds (1/8 protein)

1/2oz Chia seeds (1/4 protein)

Pinch of each: Cinnamon, cloves, ginger, nutmeg, allspice, sea salt, vanilla extract

2oz Banana (1/3 fruit)

Directions: Preheat oven to 350. Mash banana, cinnamon, flax and oats. Press mixture into a oven safe dish. Chop apple and sauté over med heat 1-2min. Add vanilla, spices and chia seeds to cooked apple and mix. Pour mixture over banana oat crust and bake 20min.

I had my Raw-nola on top of 4oz Plain Greek yogurt with 4oz Blueberries.

Raw-nola

Ingredients:

1/2oz Nuts (pecans, walnuts, almonds) (1/4 protein)

1/2oz total: Ground flax seed, chia seeds (1/4 protein)

1/2tsp Cinnamon

Sea salt

1oz Uncooked oats (full grain)

2oz Banana (1/3 fruit)

Directions: Add nuts, flax, chia seeds, cinnamon and sea salt to a food processor and pulse until nuts are small pieces. In a separate bowl mash banana and mix all ingredients together.

Side with 4oz fruit, and ½ protein for a complete breakfast

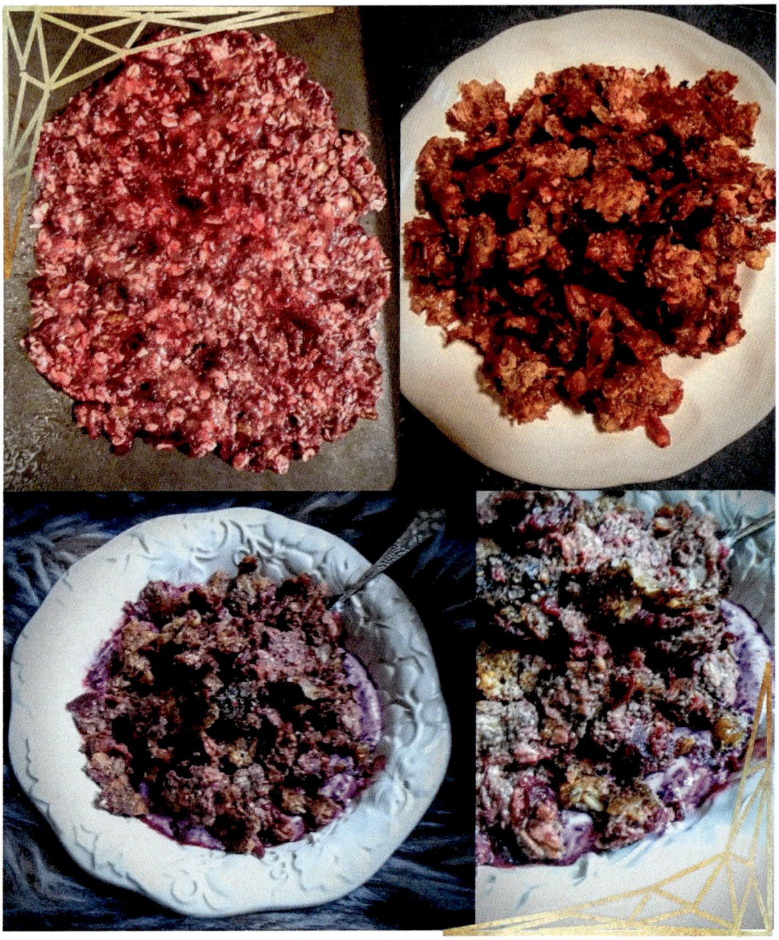

Hot Pink Granola

Ingredients:

2oz Canned beets (1/3 fruit)

1oz Uncooked oats (full grain)

2oz Banana (1/3 fruit)

1/2oz Nuts (pecans, walnuts, almonds etc)(1/4 protein)

Pinch of each: Sea salt, vanilla extract

1/2oz total: Ground flax seed, chia seeds (1/4 protein)

1/4cup Whipped aquafaba

Directions: Preheat oven to 350. Mix dry ingredients. Whip aquafaba (juice from canned chickpeas) until soft peaks form (about 10-15min). In a separate bowl mash banana, then fold in vanilla and whipped aquafaba. Pour banana mixture over dry ingredients and stir. Bake 23-28min

Side with 2oz fruit and ½ protein for a complete breakfast

Crunchy granola with roasted apples!

Apple Granola

Ingredients:

1oz Uncooked oats (full grain)

3oz Apple (1/2 fruit)

1oz total: Almonds, pecans, walnuts (1/2 protein)

1tsp Cinnamon

Pinch of each: Sea salt, vanilla extract

1/4cup Aquafaba

Directions: Preheat oven to 350. Add nuts to a food processor and pulse until nuts are small pieces. Dice apple. Whip aquafaba (juice from canned chickpeas) until soft peaks form (about 10-15min). Mix all ingredients together and bake 20min. Stir occasionally until light golden.

Side with 1/2 protein and ½ fruit for a complete breakfast

Peanut buttery delicious!

Peanut Butter Banana Granola Bars

Ingredients:

1oz Uncooked oats (full grain)

2oz Peanut butter (full protein)

3oz Banana (1/2 fruit)

Sea salt

Directions: Mash banana. Mix all ingredients together. Press mixture into a small dish and sprinkle with salt. Freeze 30min or overnight to set.

Side or top with 3oz fruit for a complete breakfast.

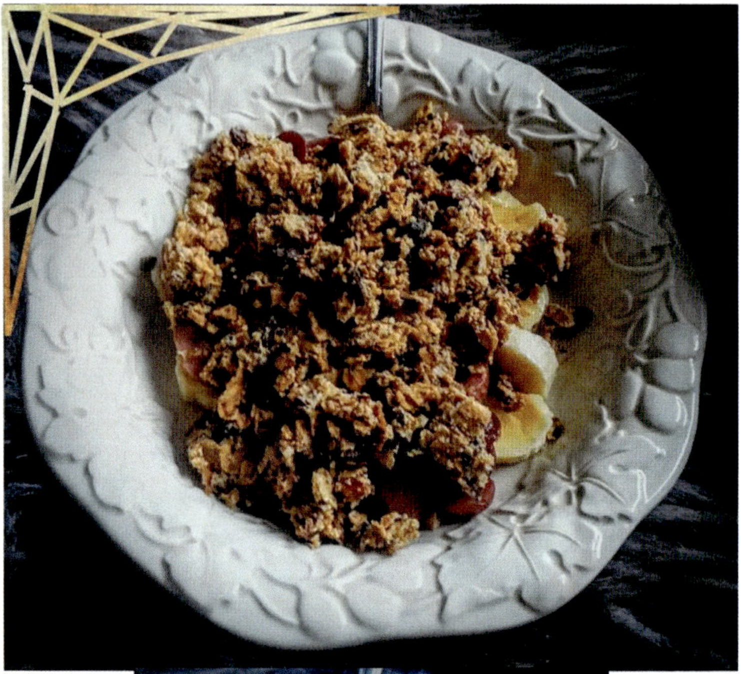

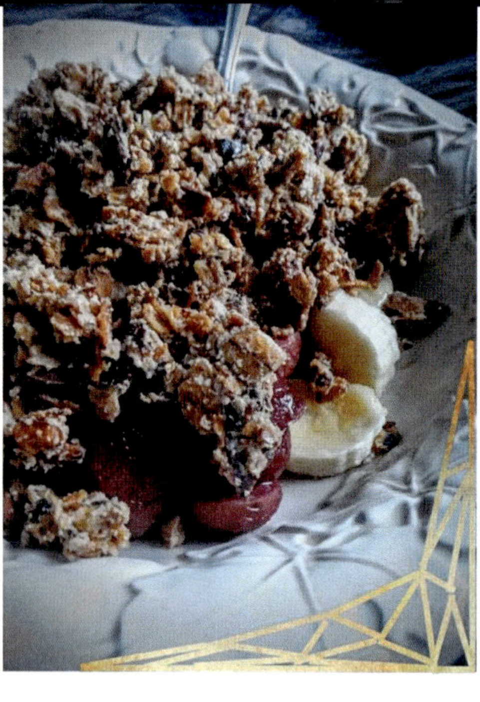

Peanut Butter Toasty Granola

Ingredients:

1oz Uncooked oats (full grain)

1oz Nuts (almonds, flax seed, sesame seeds, pecans etc.) (1/2 protein)

1oz Peanut butter (1/2 protein)

1/4cup Aquafaba

Sea salt

Directions: Preheat oven to 350. Line a baking sheet with parchment paper (or use a nonstick pan). Roast nuts and oats 13-15min or until golden. Stir occasionally. Add pecans and sesame seeds the last 5min. In a saucepan, add peanut butter and aquafaba (juice from a can of chickpeas). Set to medium heat 3-4min until mixture is pourable. Mix roasted nuts and peanut butter mixture. Pack/press mixture very hard into a small dish. Sprinkle with salt and freeze 30min to set. Break up granola and serve over fruit.

Side with 6oz fruit for a complete breakfast

Savory, filling, and you get fruit on the side!

Sweet Potato Black Bean Burger

Ingredients:

4oz Sweet potato (full grain)

1/2oz Ground flax seed (1/4 protein)

3Tbsp Water

3oz Black beans (1/2 protein)

1oz Quinoa (1/4 protein)

1Tbsp Parsley

1tsp Chili powder

1/2tsp of each: Cumin, oregano

1/8tsp Garlic salt

1/4tsp Sea salt

1Tbsp Lemon or lime juice

Directions: Mix ground flax seed and water, let sit 3-5min to thicken. Mash black beans leaving a few intact. Mix/mash cooked sweet potato, cooked quinoa, flax gel, spices and lemon juice. Fry patties 5-7min, flip and cook 5 more min. Repeat with rest of mixture.

Side with 6oz fruit for a complete breakfast

Lunch

Lunch = 1 protein, 1 fruit (6oz), 6oz vegetables, and 1 fat.

What do I do when I am having food cravings or temptations?

Baking food you should not eat when you are alone and hungry is never a good idea! I was baking some cookies (not the healthy kind), breads, and brownies for a bake sale. I was alone in the kitchen at 1am, tired, and had a long day. The house smelled soooooo good from all of the baking and I was packaging the goods (or should I call them the "bads" haha). BAD COMBO! My brain was telling me, "Oh look a delicious crumb… you had a long day… you deserve a little something… just a crumb wouldn't hurt… no one would know." My mother (who has changed her eating life-style with me) told me these wise words that changed my whole thinking! She said, "You know… that one cookie would only satisfy for maybe 5 minutes and then you would just want more. And then you would want something else after that." It's true! It was never, "I'll just have a bite and be perfectly happy." No, it was, "Wow that was sugary.. I NEED MORE!!!! I NEED TO EAT THE WHOLE WORLD!" That's what sugar does to you, it is addicting. It's said that processed sugar is more addicting than cocaine, and I believe it!

Some good things to tell yourself when you are being tempted are: "That's not my food," "Skinny feels better," "I've had that before," "That will only last 5 minutes and then I will just want more." Another thing I tell myself is that if I take one bite I won't be satisfied and I will do it again, and again, and again. It will give me license to cheat! I will feel worse, guilty, and I will have to detox from those bad sugars (when I cut out sugar at the beginning the detox lasted 2 WHOLE WEEKS! IT WAS HORRIBLE!!) I do not ever want to go through that again.

Make a 6 step craving crusher escape plan!

1. Social connection (you are less likely to binge when others are around)
2. Meditation (this does not mean to clear your mind. To meditate means to think on something, meditate the Bible, apply those scriptures to yourself personally, it will change your life!)
3. Prayer (praying for others makes it even better)
4. Gratitude (grateful hearts don't over eat.)

5. Service (don't think about yourself. Serving others will give you more satisfaction than eating something you shouldn't)

6. Distraction (do something with those hands and mind!)

   I didn't take that bite and I didn't eat any crumbs! I packaged those foods. I watched them sell the next day and it gave me more satisfaction than eating them and feeling horrible, sugar crazed and guilty.

Sin will take you farther than you want to go, keep you longer than you want to stay, and cost you more than you want to pay.

   You might be thinking, "This is going to be too hard. I can't live without sugar and flower forever! I'm not strong enough to resist those temptations." You do not have to go on this journey and life change alone. God wants us to be free from anything that will hold us in guilt and shame because He loves us.

Matthew 11:28-30

²⁸ *Come unto me, all ye that labour and are heavy laden, and I will give you rest.*

²⁹ *Take my yoke upon you, and learn of me; for I am meek and lowly in heart: and ye shall find rest unto your souls.*

³⁰ *For my yoke is easy, and my burden is light.*

If you are heavy laden with your weight and food addiction, go to God. He will help you do this. He will give you rest for your soul (your soul is your mind, will, and emotions). God wants to be involved and help us with every area of our lives, and that includes our eating habits. But we have to make the choice. God is standing at the door knocking but we must let Him in. If you do that He will help you with the cravings and temptations. He will always show you a way out because He is good and He loves you.

Revelation 3:20

Behold, I stand at the door, and knock: if any man hear my voice, and open the door, I will come in to him, and will sup with him, and he with me.

If you let Him, God will eat with you, He will be your guide. If you would like to do that say this prayer.

"God I'm sorry for letting food take over my life, and I'm sorry for trying to do this alone and failing. Please forgive me. I open the door to my heart and let you in, I believe that Jesus died on the cross to set me free from sin, sickness, guilt, addiction and shame. Help me change my eating habits, I surrender my food to You, I surrender my life to You, You are my Lord."

If you said that prayer you will be surprised how when the temptation comes, (which it will) there will be an extra force behind you helping you. That's God. When you mess up, just say you're sorry. God will be right there to pick you up, dust you off, and get you back on the right track!

With joy, Natalie

Crispy, gooey, and then dipped in peanut butter?! Yes.. Always a yes!

Cinnamon Banana Chickpea Bombs

Ingredients:

3oz Chickpea (1/2 protein)

6oz Banana (full fruit)

Pinch of each: Cinnamon, vanilla extract

1oz Peanut butter (1/2 protein)

Water

Directions: Add 3oz banana, chickpeas, vanilla, cinnamon, and blend with a hand blender (or use a fork). Slice 3oz banana. Place 1 banana slice inside your chickpea dough, fry in an oiled pan 3-4 min or until crispy, flip and repeat. In a separate bowl add peanut butter and 1Tbsp hot water, stir until smooth (repeat until desired consistency). Dip bombs into peanut butter

Side with 1 fat and 6oz vegetables for a complete lunch

Delicious to dip celery and apple slices in! Or just eat it plain.

Chickpea Cookie Dough

Ingredients:

3oz Chickpeas (1/2 protein)

1oz Peanut butter (1/2 protein)

4oz Banana (2/3 fruit)

Cinnamon

Directions: Add all ingredients in a food processor and process until smooth. Place in fridge (or freeze) for a couple hours.

Side with 2oz fruit, a fat, and 6oz vegetables for a complete lunch

These are extra yummy if you leave them in the fridge overnight!

Chickpea Blondies

Ingredients:

3oz Canned chickpeas (1/2 protein)

1oz Peanut butter (1/2 protein)

4oz Banana (2/3 fruit)

Optional- 2oz Frozen blueberries (1/3 fruit)

Pinch of each: Baking powder, baking soda, sea salt, vanilla extract

Directions: Preheat oven to 350°. Add all ingredients in a food processor (except frozen blueberries) mix until smooth or blend all ingredients except fruit until smooth then add banana and mash/mix. Stir in frozen blueberries. (You can mix these into your blondies or have them on the side.) Pour mixture into a small oiled oven safe baking dish and Bake for 25-30min. Sprinkle with sea salt.

Side with 6oz veggie and a fat, for a complete lunch

Who needs sugar when you have these!! These are surprisingly filling.

Chickpea Cookies

Ingredients:

3oz Canned chickpeas (1/2 protein)

1oz Peanut butter (1/2 protein)

4oz Banana (2/3 fruit)

2oz Frozen strawberries (Or whatever fruit you want) (1/3 fruit)

Pinch of each: Baking powder, baking soda, sea salt, vanilla extract

Directions: Preheat oven to 350°. In a food processor blend all ingredients (except strawberries) or blend all ingredients except fruit until smooth then add banana and mash/mix. Place on an oiled baking sheet and Bake for 25-30min. While still hot, sprinkle with sea salt. In a separate bowl microwave frozen strawberries 30sec-1min. Top blondies with strawberries.

Side with 6oz vegetables and a fat, for a complete lunch

Now that's refreshing!

Key lime Chia Drops

Ingredients:

6 Key limes

1oz Chia seeds (1/2 protein)

3oz Chickpea (1/2 protein)

4oz Banana (2/3 fruit)

Pinch of each: Baking powder, baking soda, sea salt, vanilla extract

Directions: Preheat oven to 350. Zest two key limes. Cut and juice 6 key limes, add chia seeds. Swirl mixture and let sit 1-2min to thicken. Add the remaining ingredients, use a hand blender or a fork and some muscle, and mix. Drop mixture onto an oiled pan and bake for 25-30.min

Side with a fat, 2oz fruit, and 6oz vegetables for a complete lunch

Flakey, Crispy, and so so delicious!

Apple Chickpea Cinnamon Rolls

Ingredients:

3oz Chickpeas (1/2 protein)

1oz Peanut butter (1/2 protein)

1oz Banana (1/6 fruit)

Pinch of each: Baking soda, baking powder, salt, vanilla extract

5oz Apple (5/6 fruit)

Cinnamon

Directions: Preheat oven to 350. Blend or use a fork and some muscle to mix all ingredients except apples and cinnamon. Sandwich chickpea mixture between 2 pieces of parchment paper and roll thin, sprinkle with cinnamon. Chop apples and place on flattened dough. Use parchment paper to roll everything up. Cut into separate rolls, place whole parchment paper with rolls onto a pan and bake 20-25 min.

Side with 1 fat and 6oz vegetables for a complete lunch

Cinnamon deliciousness!!

Chickpea Banana Cinnamon Rolls

Ingredients:

3oz Chickpeas (1/2 protein)

1oz Peanut butter (1/2 protein)

1oz Banana (1/6 fruit)

Pinch of each: Baking soda, baking powder, sea salt, vanilla extract, cinnamon

5oz Banana (5/6 fruit)

Directions: Preheat oven to 350. Blend or use a fork and some muscle to mix all ingredients except 5oz banana and cinnamon. Sandwich chickpea mixture between 2 pieces of parchment paper and roll thin, sprinkle with cinnamon. Chop banana and place on flattened dough. Use parchment paper to roll everything up. Cut into separate rolls, place whole parchment paper with rolls onto a pan and bake 20-25 min.

Side with 1 fat and 6oz vegetables for a complete lunch

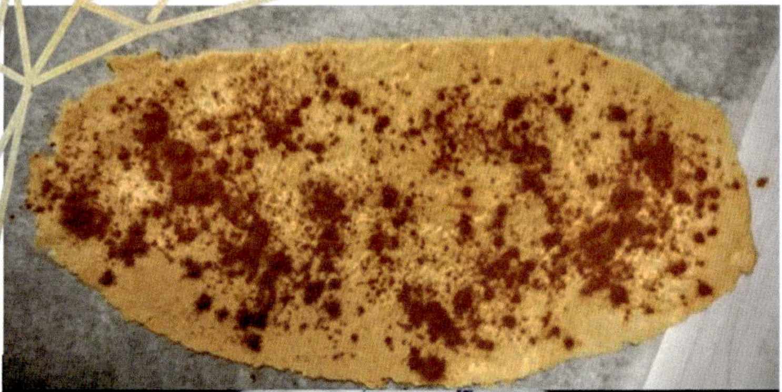

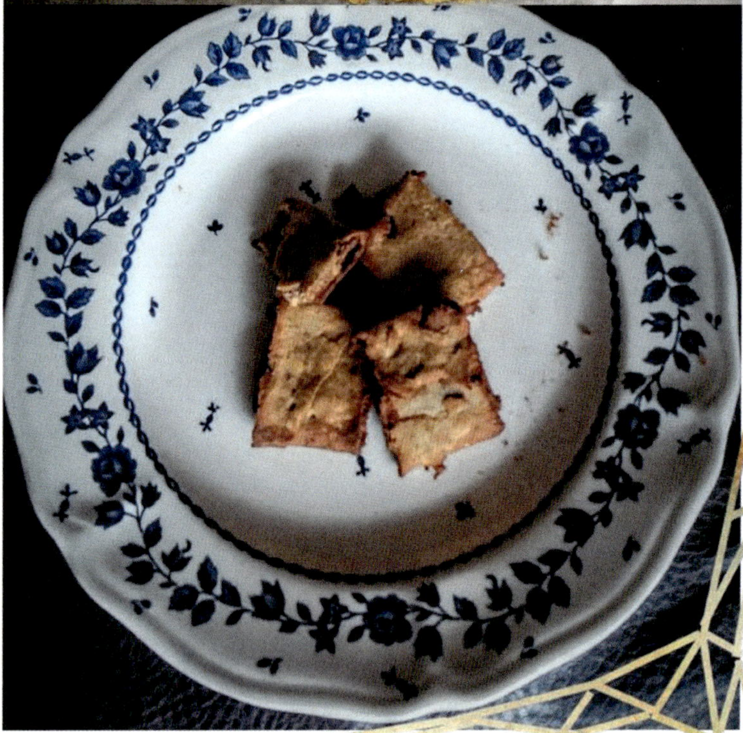

Chickpea Cinnamon Rolls

Ingredients:

3oz Chickpeas (1/2 protein)

1oz Peanut butter (1/2 protein)

1oz Banana (1/6 fruit)

Pinch of each: Baking soda, baking powder, sea salt, vanilla extract, cinnamon

Directions: Preheat oven to 350. Blend or use a fork and some muscle to mix all ingredients. Sandwich chickpea mixture between 2 pieces of parchment paper and roll thin, sprinkle with cinnamon. Use parchment paper to roll everything up. Cut into separate rolls, place whole parchment paper with rolls onto a pan and bake 20-25 min.

Side with 1 fat, 5oz fruit and 6oz vegetables for a complete lunch

Bakeing fruit gives a very different flavor and texture

Chickpea Fruit Pies

Ingredients:

3oz Chickpeas (1/2 protein)

5oz total: Apple jam*, blueberries, strawberries, banana (5/6 fruit)

Pumpkin pie spice

1oz Banana (1/6 fruit)

Pinch Sea salt

Directions: Preheat oven to 350. Blend chickpeas until smooth, mash banana and mix with chickpeas and salt. Spread mixture onto baking pan lined with parchment paper. Top crusts with fruits and sprinkle with pumpkin pie spice, bake 20min.

Side with 6oz vegetable, ½ a protein and a fat for a complete lunch

Sweet and filling

Carrot Spice Slaw

Ingredients:

3oz Banana (1/2 fruit)

6oz Shredded carrots (full vegetable)

Pinch of each: Sea salt, vanilla extract, maple extract, lemon juice

1tsp Cinnamon

1/2tsp Nutmeg

1/4tsp Ginger

1/8tsp Allspice

1Tbsp Hot water

Directions: Mash banana and mix with carrots, spices, and extracts. Pour into a small pot. Add water, splash of lemon juice and sauté 5-6min until carrots are slightly tender. Pour mixture into an airtight container and refrigerate a couple hours or overnight for best flavor.

Side with 3oz fruit, a protein and a fat for a complete lunch

Flaky peanut butter crust with apples are a YES!

Apple Pie with Peanut Butter Chickpea Crust

Ingredients:

3oz Chickpeas (1/2 protein)

1oz Peanut butter (1/2 protein)

1tsp Cinnamon

Pinch of each: Sea salt, vanilla extract, baking powder, baking soda, maple extract

1/3cup warm water

1/2tsp of each: Ginger, nutmeg

1/8tsp Allspice

Directions: Preheat oven to 375. Blend chickpeas, peanut butter, baking soda, baking powder, maple extract and sea salt. Press dough into a small oiled oven safe dish and bake 8-10min. Add cinnamon and vanilla to a small pot and heat on med/low. Dice apple, add rest of ingredients to pot and simmer 10min. Add apple mixture to crust and refrigerate 30min- overnight.

Side with 1 fat and 6oz vegetables for a complete lunch

Variety is the spice of life
You could also make this into one big pie.

Mini Pies

Ingredients:

3oz Chickpeas (1/2 protein)

1oz Peanut butter (1/2 protein)

Pinch of each: Baking soda, sea salt, baking powder, pumpkin pie spice, cinnamon, all spice

6oz Pumpkin (full vegetable)

6oz total: Apple, blueberries, cranberry sauce*, banana

Directions: Preheat oven to 350. Blend chickpeas, peanut butter, baking soda, sea salt, and baking powder. Press mixture into 4 small pie shapes onto a parchment paper lined baking sheet. In a separate bowl mix banana, 1/2 of pumpkin, pumpkin pie spice, a pinch of allspice and scoop onto the 1st piecrust. In a separate bowl, mix diced apple, rest of pumpkin and cinnamon and scoop onto the 2nd piecrust. Add diced apple and top with cranberry sauce onto the 3rd piecrust. On the 4th piecrust, add blueberries. Bake 20min.

Side with a fat for a complete lunch

*Find easy cranberry sauce in "Sauces, Seasonings, and Sides"

Peanut buttery goodness!

Peanut butter Chia Bites

Ingredients:

1/2oz Chia seeds (full fat)

2oz Peanut butter (full protein)

3oz Banana (1/2 fruit)

Pinch of each: Sea salt, vanilla extract.

Directions: Preheat oven to 350. Mix and mash all ingredients together. Scoop mixture onto a parchment paper lined baking pan. Bake 8-10min.

Side with 3oz fruit and 6oz vegetables for a complete lunch

Delicious nutty protein bites! Great for on the go

Sesame Protein Balls

Ingredients:

1oz Peanut butter (1/2 protein)

7/8oz total: Chia seeds, hemp seeds, ground flax seeds 1/8oz sesame seeds (1/2 protein)

1oz Banana (1/6 fruit)

Sea salt

Directions: Mash banana and mix all ingredients except sesame seeds. Sprinkle sesame seeds and more sea salt onto a plate. Scoop peanut butter nut mixture onto hands and roll into balls. Roll balls onto sesame seeds. Freeze or refrigerate 15min to firm.

Side with 5oz fruit, 1 fat and 6oz vegetables for a complete lunch

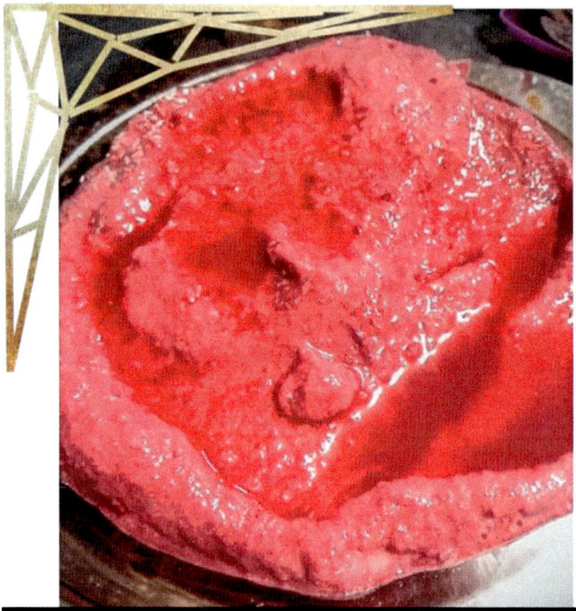

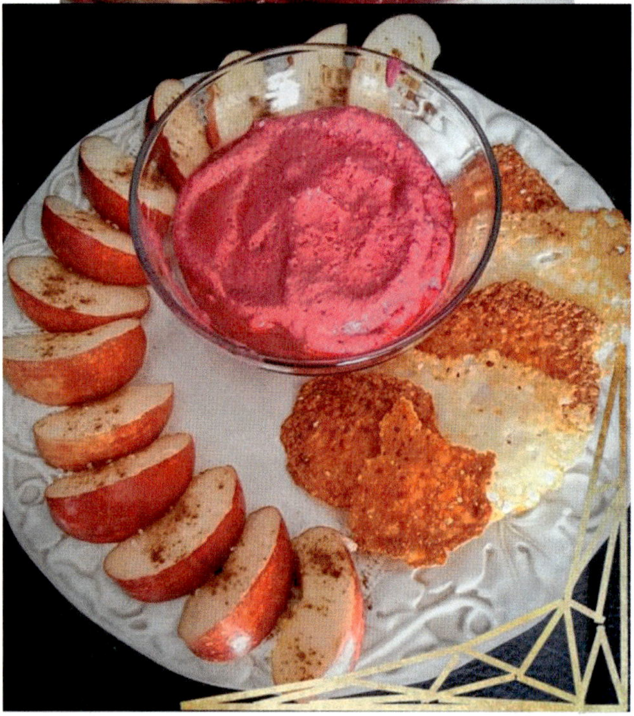

Hot Pink Beet Hummus

Ingredients:

6oz canned Beets (full vegetable)

1oz Tahini (1/2 protein)

2tbsp Lemon juice

1 clove Garlic

Directions: Add all ingredients to a food processor or blender. Process until smooth.

Side with a fat, ½ protein and 6oz fruit for a complete lunch

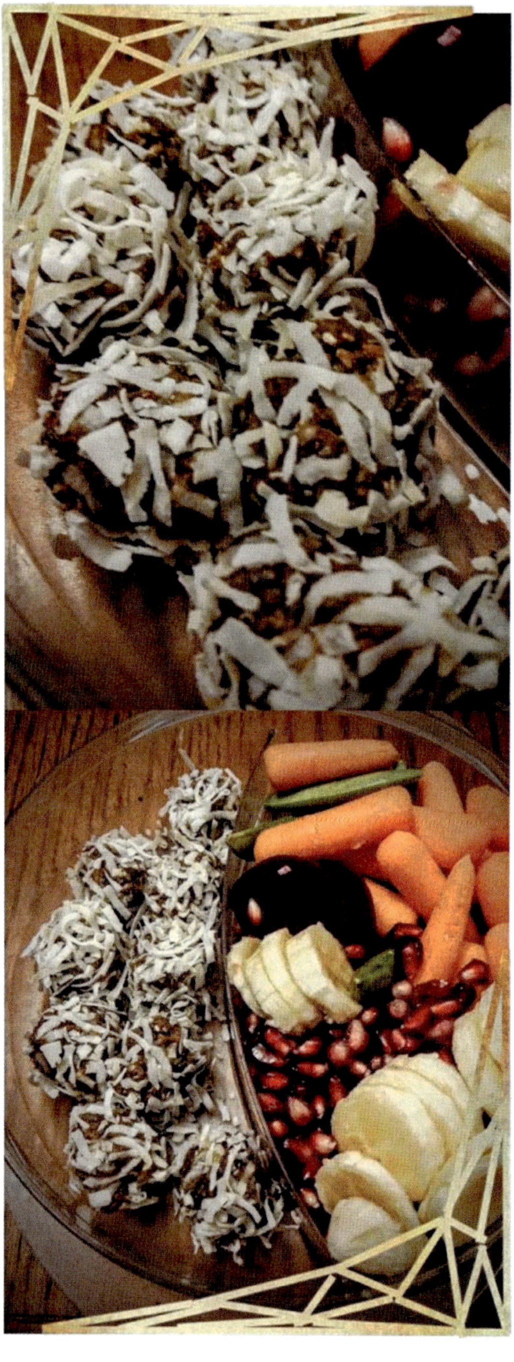

Coconut Protein Balls

Ingredients:

1oz Peanut butter (1/2 protein)

1oz Total: Chia seeds, hemp seeds, ground flax seeds (1/2 protein)

1oz banana (1/6 fruit)

Sea salt

1/2oz Unsweetened coconut flakes (full fat)

Directions: Mash banana. Add all ingredients except coconut flakes and mix. Scoop mixture into hands and roll into balls. Pour coconut flakes onto a plate and roll balls into coconut. Freeze or refrigerate 15-30min for coconut balls to firm.

Side with 5oz fruit and 6oz vegetables for a complete lunch

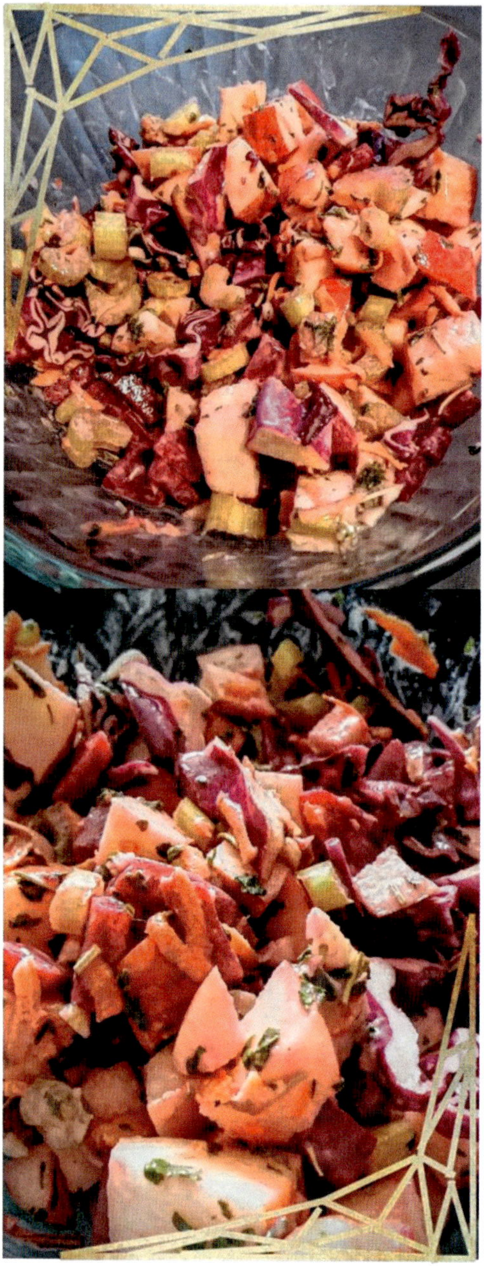

This is loaded with delicious flavor!

Red Beet Slaw with Rosemary Tahini Dressing

Ingredients:

6os total: Cabbage, celery, canned beets, carrots (full vegetable)

6oz Apple (full fruit)

1Tbsp Parsley

Rosemary tahini dressing (fat)

Directions: Shred carrots and cabbage. Finely chop beets, celery and fruit. Add rosemary dressing and mix.

Side with a protein for a complete lunch

Find Rosemary Tahini Dressing in "Sauces, Seasonings, and Sides."

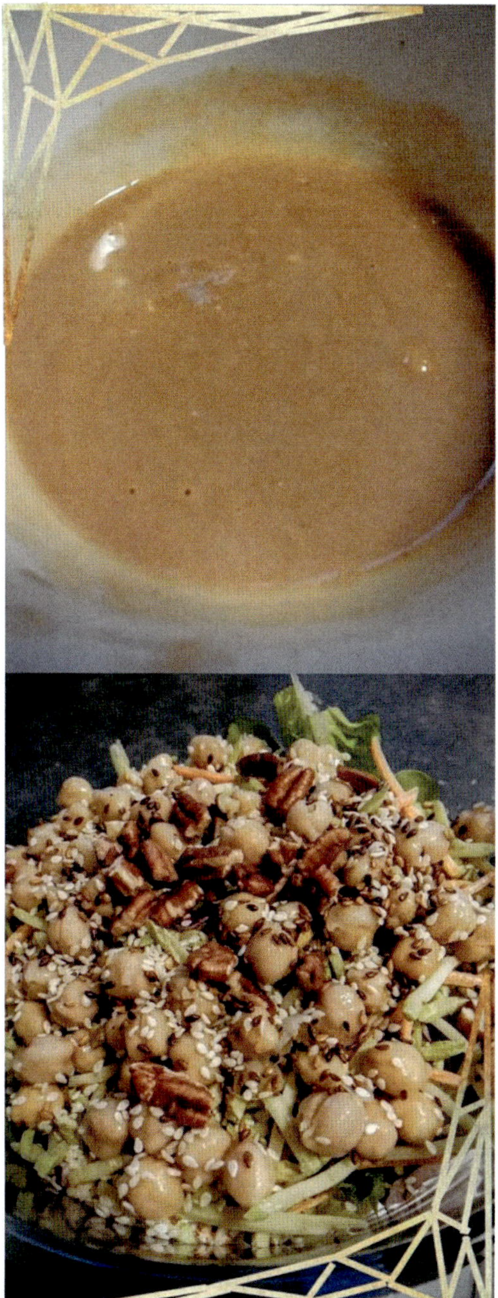

Ginger Chickpea Asian Salad

Ingredients:

1/2oz Tahini (1/4 protein)

1tsp Ginger

2 cloves Garlic

2tsp Lemon juice

1tsp of each: Apple cider vinegar, balsamic vinegar

1Tbsp Toasted sesame oil (fat)

3oz Chickpeas (1/2 protein)

1/2oz Pecans (1/4 protein)

6oz total: Romaine lettuce, broccoli slaw, onion, cabbage, shredded carrots

6oz total: Orange, pomegranate seeds (full fruit)

Directions: Mince garlic cloves and add ginger, tahini, lemon juice, apple cider vinegar, balsamic vinegar and mix. In a separate bowl chop and dice veggies. Peal and break orange into small pieces. Add fruit to veggies and top with chickpeas and nut. Pour dressing onto salad and toss. Garnish with sesame seeds.

Layers of deliciousness

B&B Blondie Bars

Ingredients:

3oz Chickpeas (1/2 protein)
1/2oz Peanut butter (full fat)
3oz Banana (1/2 fruit)
Pinch of each: Baking soda, sea salt, vanilla extract
3oz Black beans (1/2 protein)
3oz Banana (1/2 fruit)
1/4cup Aquafaba

Directions: Preheat oven to 350. Blend chickpeas, peanut butter, baking soda, sea salt, and vanilla. Mash banana and mix into blended chickpeas. In a separate bowl, whip aquafaba until soft peaks form (about 10-15min). Blend black beans until smooth. Mash banana. Mix banana, black beans, whipped aquafaba, baking soda, sea salt, and vanilla. Pour black bean mixture into a medium baking dish. Pour chickpea mixture into the middle of black bean mixture. Top with a sprinkle of sea salt and bake 35-40min until a toothpick comes out clean.

Side with 6oz vegetables for a complete lunch

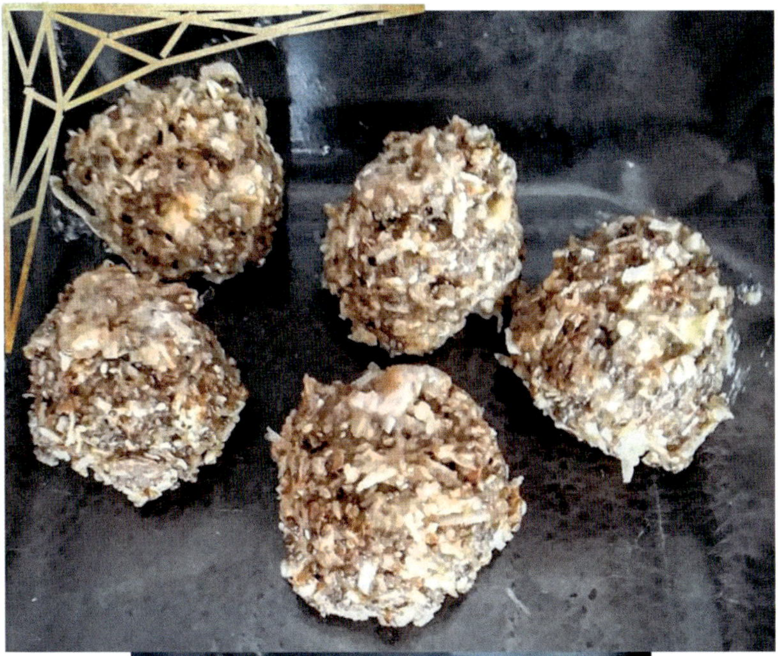

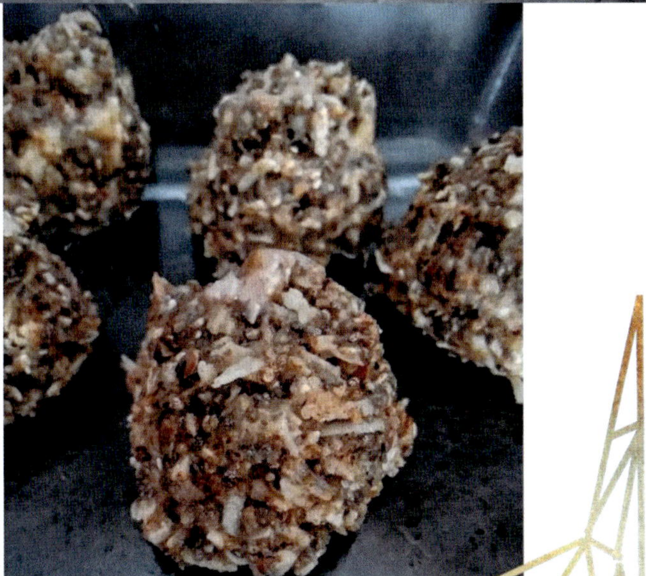

Coconut Tahini Flax Bites

Ingredients:

1/2oz Unsweetened shredded coconut (full fat)

1oz total: Ground flax seed, chia seed (1/2 protein)

1oz Tahini (1/2 protein)

Sea salt

1/4tsp Cinnamon

2oz Banana (1/3 fruit)

Directions: Mash banana. Mix all ingredients together. Scoop mixture into hands and roll into balls. Freeze 30min to set.

Side with 6oz vegetables and 4oz fruit for a complete lunch

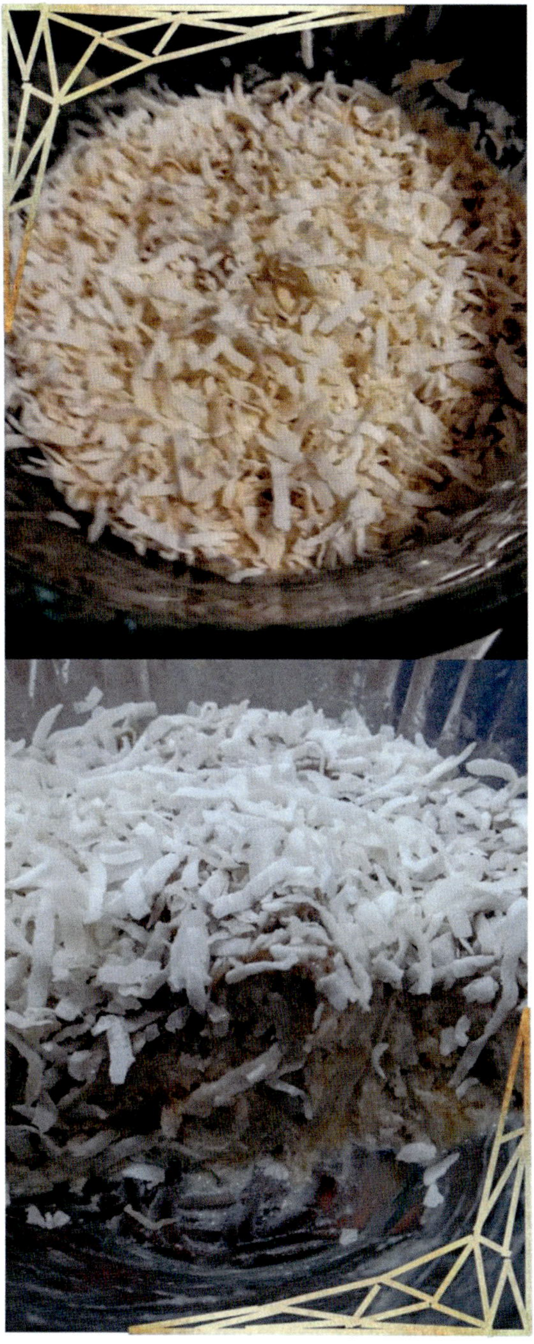

Coconut Tahini Soft Serve

Ingredients:

6oz Banana (full fruit)

2oz Tahini (full protein) (you can also use peanut butter)

Sea salt

1/2oz Unsweetened shredded coconut (full fat)

Directions: Mash banana. Mix tahini, ½ coconut, banana and salt. Top with the rest of coconut and freeze 2-3hours.

Side with 6oz vegetables for a complete lunch

Dinner

Dinner = 1 protein, 1 fat, and 14oz vegetables.

What is with food? Is food addicting or is it just me?

As I was thinking about this, God started to reveal some things about food. Let's look at the beginning. Adam and Eve. What was their first sin? Food. What was Jesus' first temptation in the wilderness? Food. (not just food… but BREAD!) The Bible has A LOT to say about food. Jesus told us in Matthew 6:25,

[25] Therefore I say unto you, Take no thought for your life, what ye shall eat, or what ye shall drink; nor yet for your body,…Is not the life more than meat…

I want to eat to live, not live to eat.

Be watchful when the devil tries to tempt you, "You work hard. You deserve some desert. Why does everyone else get to eat desert and you don't? Just try it. No one will know."

If it's selfish, makes you feel sorry for yourself, sneaky, or will cause you guilt later, DON'T DO IT.

1 Corinthians 10:13

13 There hath no temptation taken you but such as is common to man: but God is faithful, who will not suffer you to be tempted above that ye are able; but will with the temptation also make a way to escape, that ye may be able to bear it.

Food is important to God, or He wouldn't have created us to have to eat food to live. He takes care of us, He fed the Israelites when they were in the wilderness, and food came from heaven. God had ravens bring food to Elijah. God will do the same for you when you trust Him with your life.

1 Corinthians 10:31

31 Whether therefore ye eat, or drink, or whatsoever ye do, do all to the glory of God.

The spaghetti squash absorbs the delicious flavor!

Slow Cooker Veggie Sloppy Joe

Ingredients:

1 of each: Onion, red pepper, spaghetti squash

2 Carrots

3 Cloves garlic

1 1/2Tbsp Chili powder

1/2tsp Onion powder

1/4tsp Cayenne pepper (optional)

15oz Jar spaghetti sauce

15oz Can diced tomatoes

1tsp of each: Mustard, cumin, Dijon mustard, apple cider vinegar

Directions: Chop onion, pepper, carrots, and garlic. Slice spaghetti squash in half, and scoop out seeds. Mix all ingredients except spaghetti squash in a crockpot, place spaghetti squash on top of mixture. Cook on high 4hours. Measure out 14oz plus 2oz free of just the sauce.

Side with a protein, and a fat for a complete dinner

Sauce

Side with 1/2 protein, and a fat for a complete dinner

Cabbage Egg Rolls

Ingredients:

1 Can bean sprouts

1 Sweet Vidalia Onion

2-3 cloves Garlic

1tsp each: Garlic salt, onion powder

2tsp Ginger

1/2 Cabbage (3 whole leaves)

1-2 Carrots

4oz Apple cider vinegar

3oz Water

1/2oz Balsamic vinegar

3oz Chickpeas (Or 2oz meat) (1/2 protein)

Directions: Shred cabbage and carrots. Chop onions and garlic. Sauté bean sprouts, cabbage, carrots, onion, garlic. In a separate bowl, mix apple cider vinegar, water, balsamic vinegar and spices. Pour sauce into veggies and mix, place whole cabbage leaves on top, cover and cook on med/low 15-20 min. Measure a total of 14oz cabbage leaves with cooked veggies, add chickpeas.

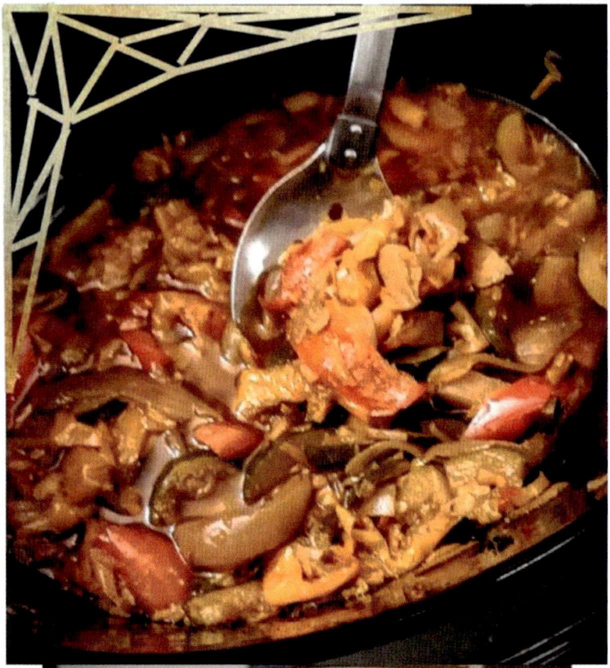

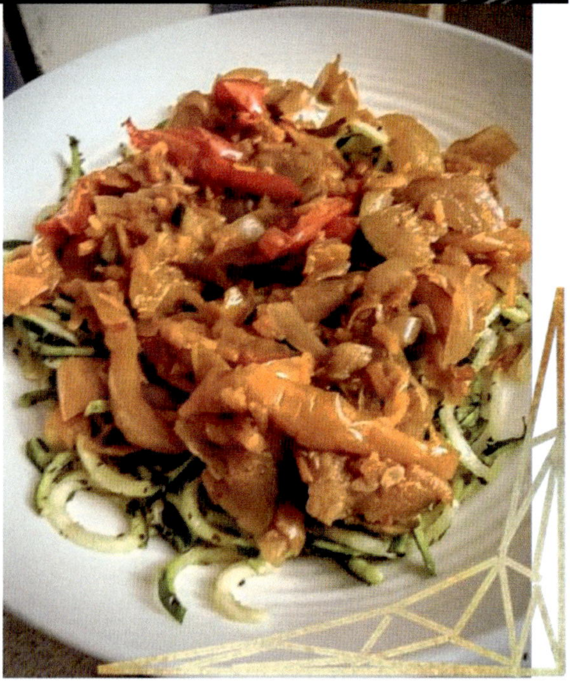

Crockpot Fajita Vegetables

Ingredients:

Onion

Colored pepper

Zucchini

1Tbsp Taco seasoning*

Directions: Chop all vegetables and add to crockpot. Sprinkle with taco seasoning and cook on high 3-4hours.

Side with a protein and a fat for a complete dinner

Find Taco seasoning in "Sauces Seasoning And Sides"

Sauces, Seasonings, and Sides

Gotta have that crunch.

Seed Crackers

Ingredients:

2½ cups total: Sunflower, pumpkin, sesame, hemp, poppy seeds, slivered almonds (Or any nuts/seeds you like.)

½ cup total: Chia and Flax seeds

1 cup Water

½ tsp Sea salt

Directions: Preheat oven to 375. Mix all ingredients together. Let sit for 10-15min to thicken. Spread out seed mixture on parchment lined baking sheet, about 1/8 in thick. Bake for 50-60min. Check crackers at 10min to make sure they are not burning, if they look like they are burning reduce heat to 350 (repeat every 15min or so because every oven is different). Let cool and break into pieces. Store in an airtight container.

2oz = 1 protein. 1/2oz = 1 fat.

Perfect to add to oatmeal, Ezekiel toast with peanut butter, or just on top of sliced apples.

Apple Banana Rhubarb Chia Jelly

Ingredients:

2 cups total: Frozen Apples, frozen banana, frozen rhubarb

1Tbsp Chia seeds

1tsp Ground flax seed

Vanilla extract

Directions: Cook chopped apples, banana, rhubarb and vanilla in a pot on medium heat for 10min. Remove pot from stove and stir in chia and flax seeds, let cool and store in fridge.

Jelly counts as a fruit

Smells like heaven!

Strawberry Rhubarb Jam

Ingredients:

2 cups total: Frozen strawberries, frozen rhubarb

1Tbsp Chia seeds

Directions: Cook rhubarb and strawberries in a pot on medium heat for 10min. Remove pot from stove and stir in chia seeds, let cool and store in fridge.

Jam counts as a fruit

Creamier than classic ranch!!!

Tahini Ranch Dressing

Ingredients:

1/2oz Tahini (full fat)

1/2oz Lemon juice

1tsp Hot water

2tsp Dill

1-2tsp Dijon mustard

1/2tsp each: Onion powder, garlic powder (or 1 clove garlic)

Sea salt, pepper

Directions: Mix all ingredients together.

Dressing counts as 1 fat

Perfect for Thanksgiving! Or a Monday...

Cauliflower Stuffing

Ingredients:

4 12oz Bags frozen cauliflower

1 Onion

2 Carrots

2 Stalks celery

1/2Cup Vegetable stock

1/4tsp Sea salt

1Tbsp each: Parsley, rosemary, sage

Directions: Chop and sauté onion, carrots and celery. Add rest of ingredients, cook on medium heat for 20min. Break up cauliflower with a spoon, and serve.

1 pan Veggies!

Squashed Brussel Sprouts Carrots and Spinach Stir Fry

Ingredients:

2 12oz bags frozen Brussel sprouts

2 12oz bags frozen Carrots

1 big handful of Spinach

1-2tsp Basil

1Tbsp Parsley

1tsp Garlic powder

Pinch of each: Garlic salt, sea salt, pepper

Directions: Lightly oil skillet, add vegetables (except spinach) seasonings, and sauté 10min. Squash Brussel sprouts. Add spinach and cook 5-10 more minutes.

So easy and still yummy

Easy Guacamole

Ingredients:

2oz Avocado (full fat)

2oz Salsa (condiment 2oz free)

1/8oz Lemon juice

Sea salt

Directions: Chop avocado and mix all ingredients together.

It's surprising how flavorful roasted nuts are compared to raw nuts!

Roasted Nuts

Ingredients:

Nuts (pecans, walnuts, almonds, or whatever nut you like)

Sea salt

Directions: Preheat oven to 400. Line a baking sheet with parchment paper, spread nuts and sprinkle with salt, bake 10-15min or until golden brown stir every couple of minutes for an even roast.

Gives your meals a little crunch

Toasted Sesame Seeds

Ingredients:

Sesame seeds

Directions: Preheat oven to 400. Line a baking sheet with parchment paper, spread seeds and bake 5-10min or until golden brown stir every couple of minutes for an even roast.

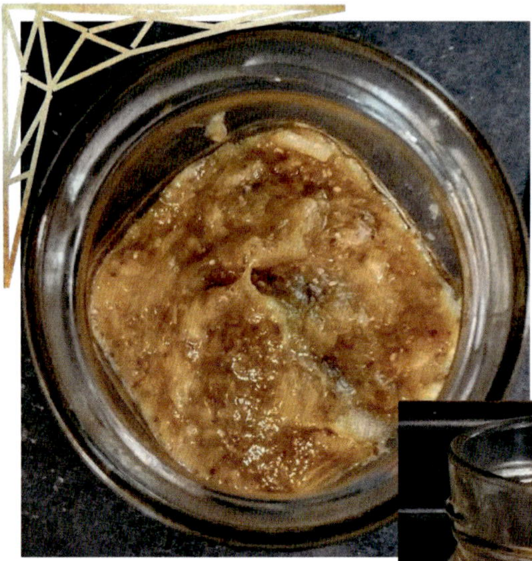

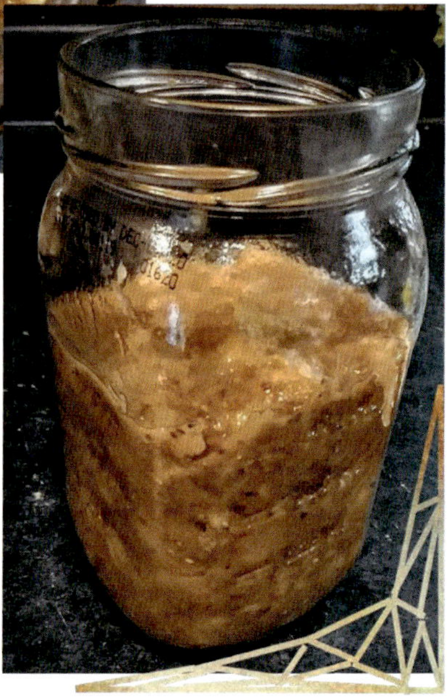

Apple Chia Jam

Ingredients:

2 cups total: Apples

1Tbsp Chia seeds

Vanilla extract

Directions: Chop apples and cook in a pot on medium heat for 10min. Remove pot from stove and stir in chia seeds, let cool and store in fridge.

Jam counts as a fruit

This will add some spice to your life!

Southwest Black Bean Hummus

Ingredients:

3oz Black beans (1/2 protein)

1/2-1tsp Chipotle pepper powder

2Tbsp Lime juice (about 2 ½ limes)

1Tbsp Parsley

1tsp Cumin

Directions: Add all ingredients to a food processor and process until smooth.

Hummus counts as 1/2 protein

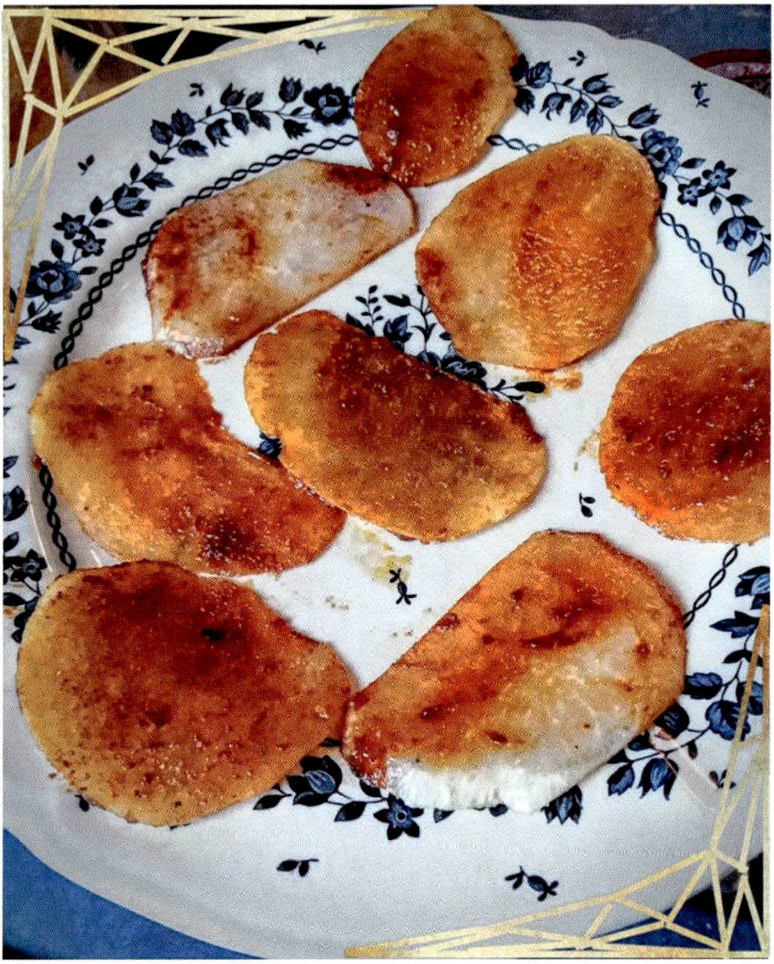

Jicama Tortillas

Ingredients:

Jicama

Paprika

Garlic salt

Directions: Thinly slice jicama with a mandolin or a vegetable slicer. Heat a skillet, add jicama slices and sprinkle with seasonings. Fry 30sec, flip and repeat with the rest of jicama slices.

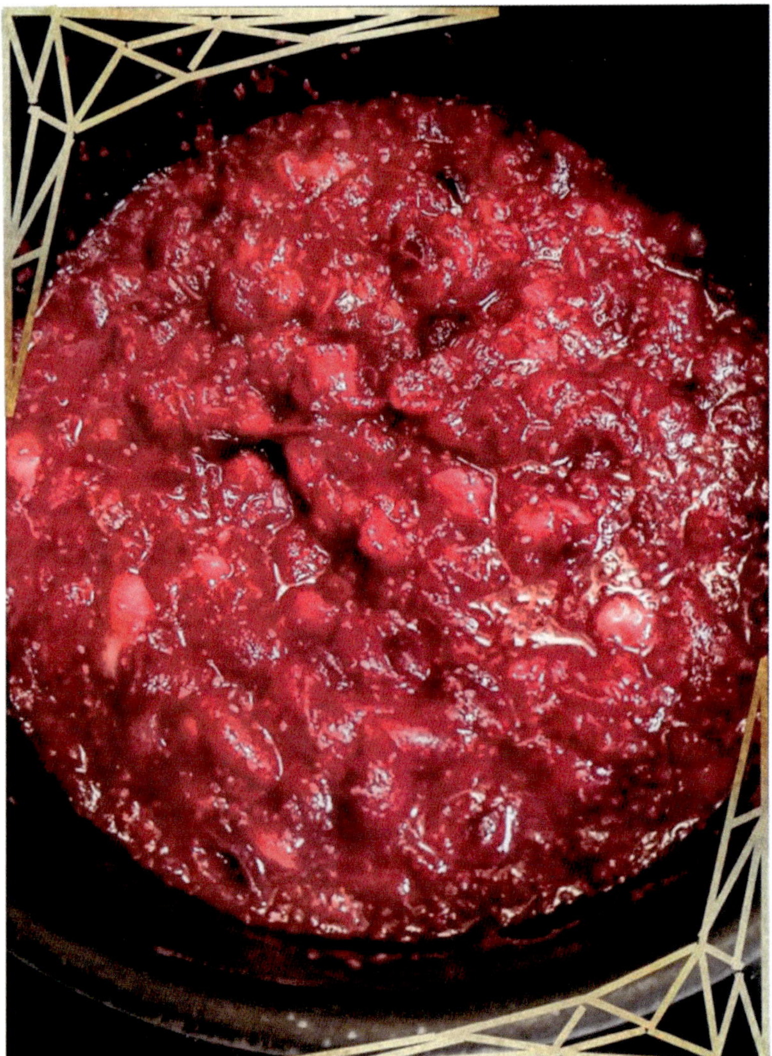

Cranberry Sauce

Ingredients:

12oz Bag of fresh cranberries

1 cup Water

1 Orange zested

¼ Banana

1 cup Crushed pineapple

1Tbsp Chia seeds

Directions: Add cranberries and water to a medium pot, bring to a boil, reduce heat and simmer 5-7min until cranberries start to break down. Add orange zest, pineapple and chopped banana. Simmer 4-5min. Add chia seeds and let cool.

Nice and crispy!

Cinnamon Roasted Squash Seeds

Ingredients:

Squash seeds

Cinnamon

Sea salt

Directions: Preheat oven to 375. Mix and add all ingredients to a baking pan and bake 10min. Shake/stir pan and roast 10min more. Repeat until seeds are golden brown and crisp.

Pink creamy tahini dressing!

Rosemary Tahini Dressing

Ingredients:

1/2oz Tahini (full fat)

1 1/2Tbsp Lemon juice

2Tsp Apple cider vinegar

1Tbsp Rosemary

1 clove Garlic

1tsp Beet juice from can

Sea salt

Directions: Mince garlic. Whisk all ingredients.

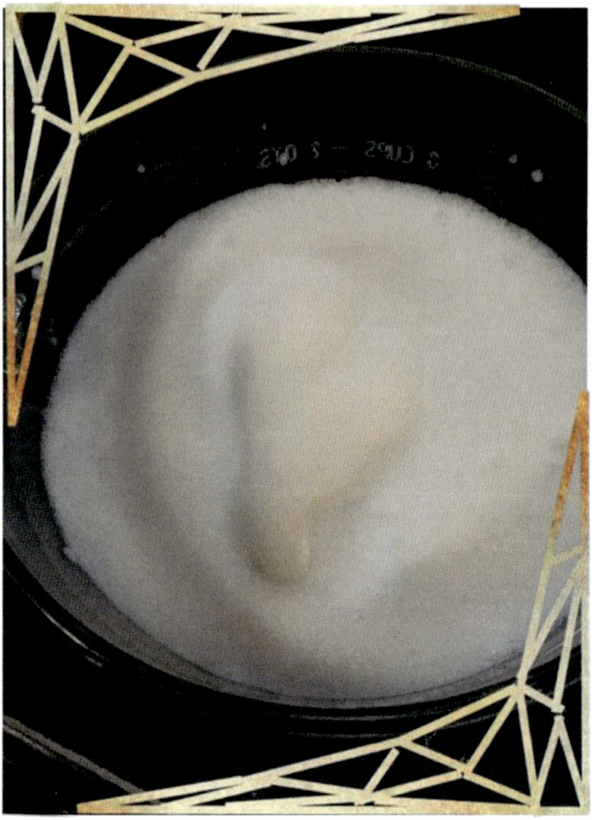

Aquafaba

Ingredients:

Juice from a can of chickpeas

Directions: Pour chickpea juice into a bowl. Use a hand blender or a freestanding mixer. Whip on med 1-2min until aquafaba starts to get frothy. Whip on high 10-15min until stiff peaks form. (If you're having problems getting your aquafaba to whip add a little cream of tartar)

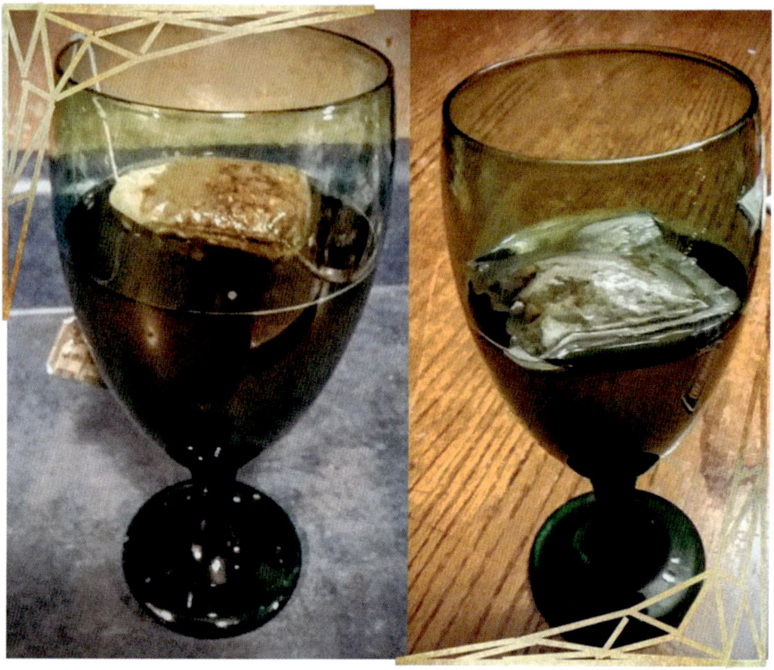

Bubble Tea

Ingredients:

Tea bag of choice

Seltzer or Plain Carbonated water

Directions: Chill carbonated water. Add tea bag to a cup and pour just enough hot water to cover tea bag. Let steep 4-5min. Swirl glass or stir with a spoon. Pour in chilled carbonated water and enjoy.

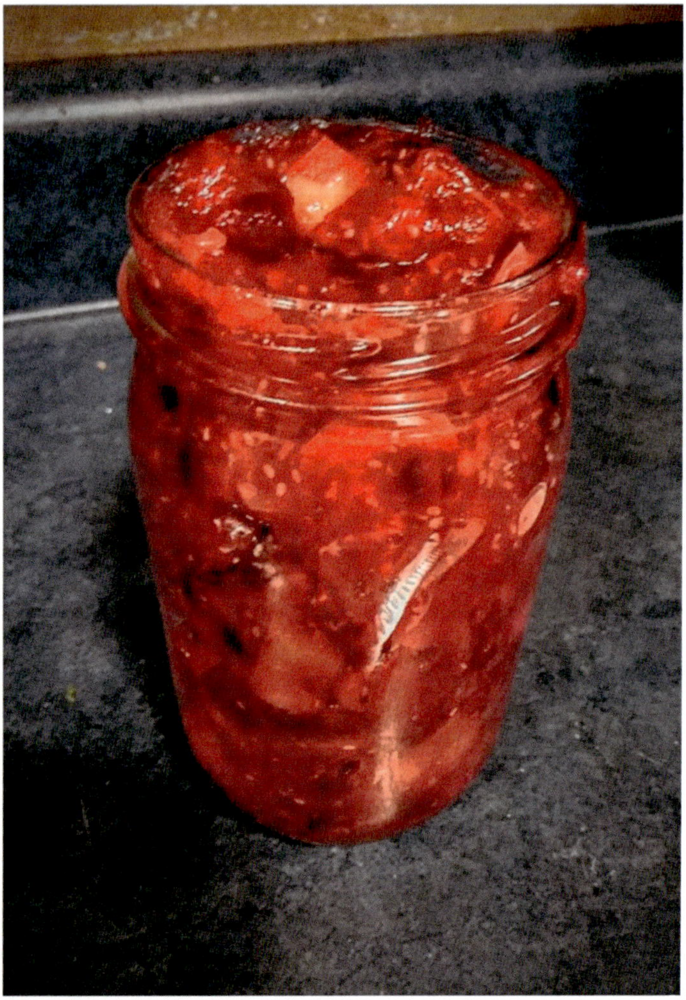

Cranberry Apple Chia Jam

Ingredients:

Cranberries

Apples

1Tbsp Chia seeds

Water

Directions: Add cranberries and 1-2cups water to a pot. Bring Cranberries to a boil. Boil 3-4min. Chop apples. Add apples to boiling cranberries. Reduce heat and simmer 10min until fruit starts to thicken. Remove from heat and add chia seeds.

6oz Jam= fruit serving

Taco Seasoning

Ingredients:

1 Tbsp. Chili powder

1/4 tsp Garlic powder, onion powder, crushed red pepper flakes, dried oregano

1/2 tsp Paprika

1 1/2 tsp Cumin

1/2 tsp Salt, pepper

Directions: Mix spices together. Add to 1Lb of beef or chicken.

Bulk Taco Seasoning

1 cup Chili powder.

4 tsp Garlic powder, onion powder, crushed red pepper flakes, dried oregano

8 tsp Paprika

½ cup Cumin

8 tsp Salt, Pepper.

A little about me.

Growing up I never knew how normal healthy people ate. I have been overweight since I was about 9 years old. I always felt insecure about my weight and eating around others. Then as a family, we changed our diets to whole, healthy foods… and I still was overweight (it is possible to eat the right food and still eat too much of it). Then slowly we went back to eating unhealthily, but just not as bad.

Before

As I grew up, I tried all the different kinds of diets with my mom and sister. They never lasted. The sugar and flour were always there… just waiting for us to fail… and we did. I even tried the keto diet and lost 10 pounds! But…I went right back to the old eating habits.

Until one day, my mom called my sister and I into her room. She showed us the first video to an amazing plan on Facebook. It talked about how this way of eating takes all the willpower out. (Which is what we needed!!) Us three girls started and went all out. Once we started, we quickly found out that this is the best lifestyle-ever!

After

For a couple of years, God had been speaking to my mom and He told her, "Your influence for Me will not be as effective in your society if you remain overweight. People will be more accepting and open if you will lose the weight." (sadly, our society is very judgmental) So that is what we did. This has been the best lifestyle change. (it is not a diet). My mom, sister, and I have lost over 80lbs each and have never felt better! The body insecurities are GONE! I don't have to think, "What are they thinking about me. Do I look fat? Will I fit in that chair? I have to shop in the plus size section while all of my friends get to shop in the cute clothing sections." Now I can just throw on jeans and a t-shirt and do not have to worry about my body. I have so much energy. I don't have tired headaches or the 'blec' feeling after eating junk food. I never have to feel insecure about eating food in front of other people. I can shop in the normal size people sections. I have never been this skinny in my whole life and I will never go back to the old me. Never! I am not at my goal weight yet but I'm enjoying the journey. I am living Deliciously Free!!

With joy, Natalie

About the Author

Natalie was born and raised in Minnesota and was home-schooled along with her siblings. She works full-time with her family at Love of God Family Church in Fergus Falls, Minnesota, leading worship, singing, playing keyboard, and drums. She also writes skits and performs with the church's Blast Kids program. She is also the founder and creator of Closet Critters.

Weightlossrecipescookbook.com

Facebook.com/weightlossrecipescookbook

60 BRAND NEW RECIPES IN VOLUME ONE!
ORDER YOURS TODAY!
WeightLossRecipesCookbook.com
Or visit Barnes & Noble online

WEIGHT LOSS RECIPES

-no sugar, no flour, made deliciously easy-

COOKBOOK

Volume 1

Natalie Aul

60 BRAND NEW RECIPES IN VOLUME TWO!
ORDER YOURS TODAY!
WeightLossRecipesCookbook.com
Or visit Barnes & Noble online

60 BRAND NEW RECIPES IN VOLUME THREE!
ORDER YOURS TODAY!
WeightLossRecipesCookbook.com
Or visit Barnes & Noble online

WEIGHT LOSS RECIPES

-no sugar, no flour, made deliciously easy-

COOKBOOK

Volume 3

Natalie Aul

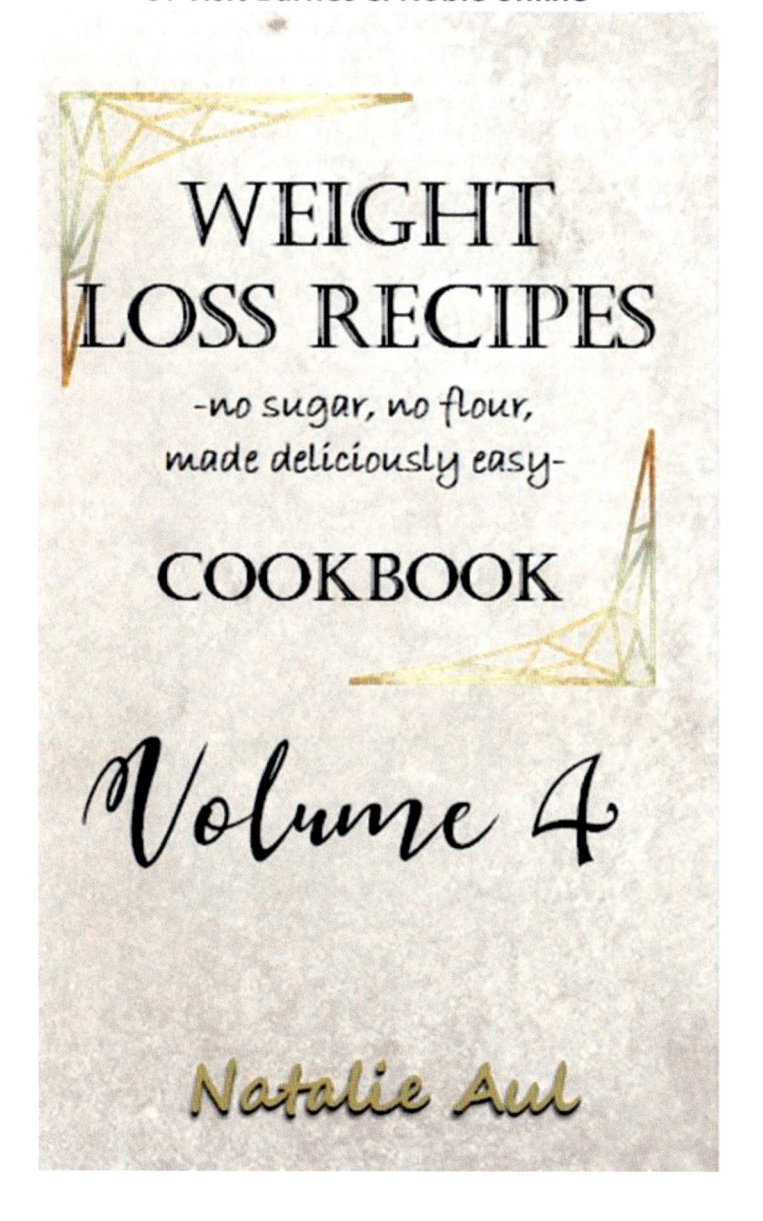

60 BRAND NEW RECIPES IN VOLUME FOUR!
ORDER YOURS TODAY!
WeightLossRecipesCookbook.com
Or visit Barnes & Noble online

WEIGHT LOSS RECIPES

-no sugar, no flour, made deliciously easy-

COOKBOOK

Volume 4

Natalie Aul

60 BRAND NEW RECIPES IN VOLUME FIVE!
ORDER YOURS TODAY!
WeightLossRecipesCookbook.com
Or visit Barnes & Noble online

60 BRAND NEW RECIPES IN VOLUME SIX!
ORDER YOURS TODAY!
WeightLossRecipesCookbook.com
Or visit Barnes & Noble online

WEIGHT LOSS RECIPES
-no sugar, no flour, made deliciously easy-

COOKBOOK

Volume 6

Natalie Aul

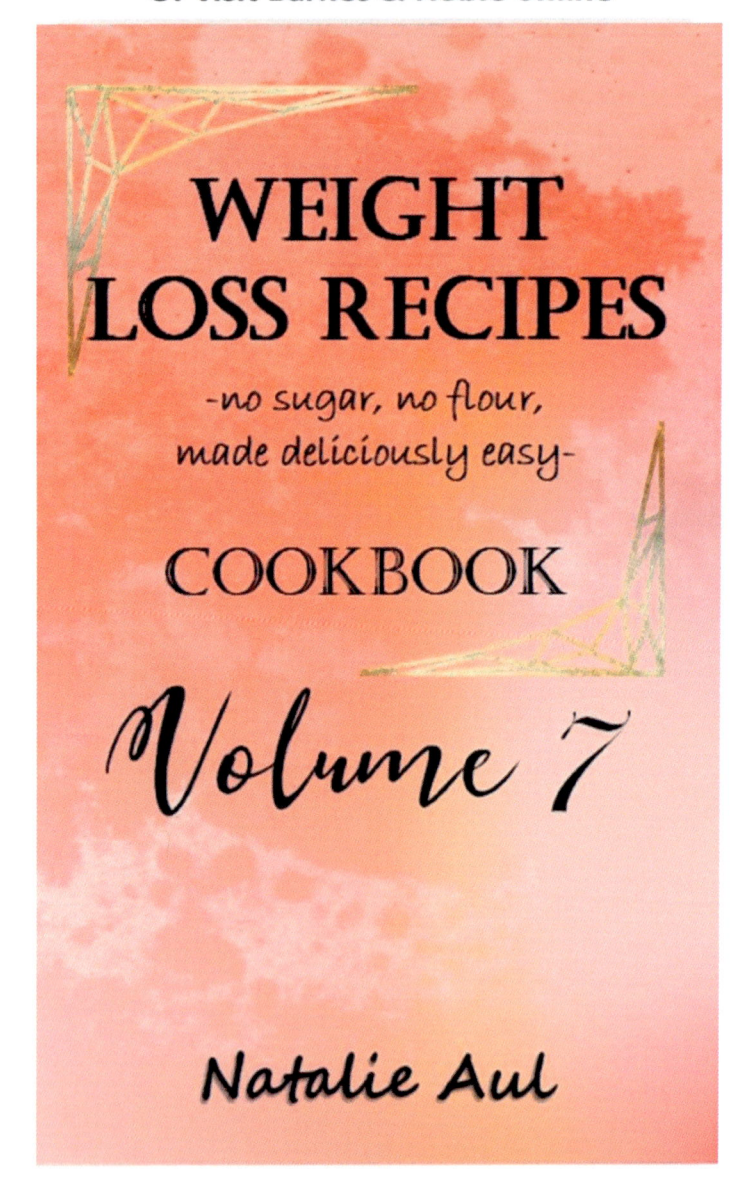

**60 BRAND NEW RECIPES IN VOLUME SEVEN!
ORDER YOURS TODAY!
WeightLossRecipesCookbook.com
Or visit Barnes & Noble online**

WEIGHT LOSS RECIPES

-no sugar, no flour, made deliciously easy-

COOKBOOK

Volume 7

Natalie Aul

Volumes 1-5 in one BIG BOOK! Over 300 recipes in one. You will love Cooking with Joy. Order yours today!
WeightLossRecipesCookbook.com
Or visit Barnes & Noble online

Finally, an affordable product everyone can use!

Our Products
We sell all natural skin and body care products with no artificial, synthetic, or GMO's. Just the very basic, wholesome ingredients you can trust.

About Our Products

We found it hard to find natural products that were actually affordable so we began to make our own products that contain very few ingredients. We found pure freedom in these products. Not only free from harmful chemicals and ingredients that we can't even pronounce but also free from the financial stress of trying to find natural products that fit into our budget.

The natural ingredients in our products are simple, basic, and essential. This simplicity and peace of mind gives you PURE FREEDOM

AULNATURAL.COM
aulnatural@yahoo.com - FACEBOOK.COM/AulNatural
218-685-4507

Christian Historical Romance Fiction Novels by
Kelly Aul

These books capture the hearts of all ages with inspiring stories filled with adventure, romance, thrilling twists, and hope. Most importantly, they are pure and appropriate for everyone.

Available in Stores:	Rescued from Worry
Trumm Drug in Elbow Lake, MN	**Never Forsaken Series**
Higher Grounds in Fergus Falls, MN	1. Audrey's Sunrise
	2. In the Midst of Darkness
Available Online:	3. Holding Faith
Amazon (ebook and paperback)	4. Everlasting
Barnes & Noble (ebook and hardcover)	**Relentless Series**
	1. Unspoken Pursuit

www.KellysCompleteDigitalDesign.com

Facebook.com/KellyAulNovels

Love of God Family Church

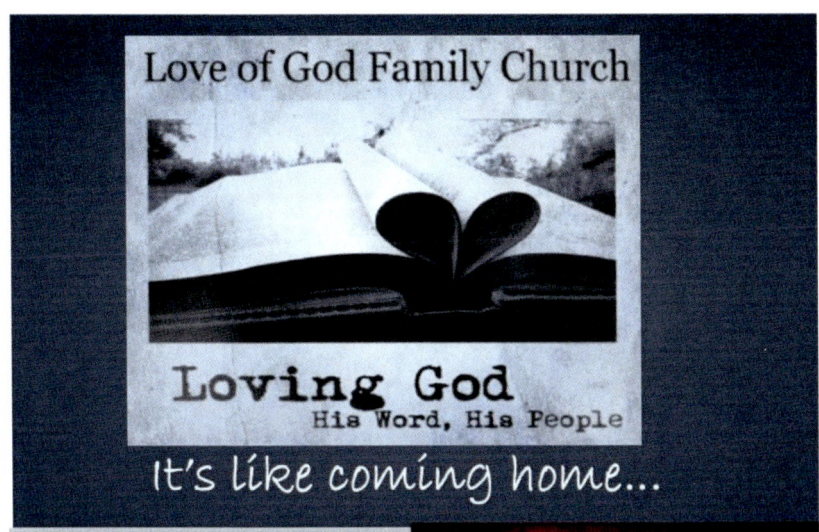

Loving God
His Word, His People

It's like coming home...

We're a family growing together in worship. We serve, laugh, play games, learn, and we share one another's victories and sorrows.

Our doors are open. Our hearts are open, also. If you're looking for a place to belong and grow close to God,

Welcome home!

Pastors Tom & Maggie Aul

www.LoveofGodFamilyChurch.com

Sunday Service   (LIVE STREAM ON FACEBOOK)
11:00am – 829 N. Tower Road, Fergus Falls, MN
Sunday Radio Program
7:30am KBRF 12.50 AM
Fergus Falls P.E.G. ACCESS TV
Sundays at 4:00pm / Mondays at 7:00pm / Fridays at 7:00am
First Sunday of Each Month
Food and fellowship after the service
The Sunday of Each Month after TAYA
(during the school year)
Service will be at 4:00pm
Tuesdays   (LIVE STREAM ON FACEBOOK)
Prayer - 5:30-6:30pm / Bible Study - 6:30-7:30pm
Wednesday Nights (LIVE STREAM ON FACEBOOK)
"BLAST" (Bible Learning And Seeking Truth) Kids Night
6:00-7:00pm for ages 3 and up—Free and free bus ride
Second Saturday of Each Month:
Gals Bible Study / 2:00-4:00pm
Guys Bible Study / 2:00-4:00pm
Third Saturday of Each Month:
TAYA (Teens And Young Adults) Games Night
YMCA in Fergus Falls, MN   - Free bus ride
6:30-10:00pm / For ages 9-25 / $4.00 to come
Forth Friday of Each Month:
TAYA FOR REAL
Free and free food, prizes, and bus ride
7:00-8:30pm / For ages 9-25
Exercise Classes
Tuesdays — Zumba 4:00pm, Bone Strengthening Exercise 4:30pm

Kelly's Complete Digital Design

GRAPHIC DESIGNER - PUBLISHER - VIDEO PRODUCTION

WHETHER YOU ARE A CHURCH, COMPANY, SMALL BUSINESS, OR WANT TO PUBLISH YOUR WORK, I WOULD LIKE TO HELP YOU, ALL THE WHILE KEEPING IT LOW COST AND AFFORDABLE. I WANT TO MAKE THE ENTIRE PROCESS AS EASY AND SIMPLE AS POSSIBLE. PLEASE CONTACT ME TODAY FOR A CONSULTATION AND QUOTE FOR WHAT YOU ARE LOOKING FOR. I LOOK FORWARD TO HELPING YOU.

KELLY

KELLYAULNOVELS.COM

FACEBOOK.COM/KELLYAULNOVELS

VIDEO PRODUCTION

Let me help you make affordable, memorable videos that capture life's priceless moments and will last for generations.

- **GRADUATION VIDEOS**
- **WEDDING VIDEOS**
- **MEMORIAL VIDEOS**
- **SLIDESHOWS**
- **VIDEO INTRO / OUTRO**
- **ADVERTISEMENT VIDEOS**
- **VIDEOS LOOPS**
- **INSTRUCTIONAL VIDEOS**
- **VHS TO DVD TRANSFER**

— PUBLISHER —

Have you written a poem, children's book, or novel but don't know how to share it with the world? Let me help! I will work with you in creating a unique and professional looking book, without it costing a fortune.

- **PUBLISH ON AMAZON BARNES & NOBLE**
- **BOOK COVERS**
- **FORMATTING**
- **EDITING**
- **EBOOKS**
- **PAPERPACK BOOKS**
- **HARDCOVER BOOKS**
- **ISBN NUMBERS**
- **EIN TAX ID NUMBERS**

GRAPHIC DESIGNER

Let me help you in all of your advertising needs, whether it's a fun event or a new business venture. I will work with you to create affordable designs that will catch everyone's eye and make a lasting impression.

- **LOGOS**
- **FLYERS**
- **BUSINESS CARDS**
- **NEWSLETTERS**
- **MAGAZINES**
- **BROCHURES**
- **COVER LETTERS**
- **POWERPOINTS**
- **PHOTO EDITING**
- **DVD/CD COVERS**
- **BASIC WEBSITE DESIGNER**
- **FACEBOOK COVER PHOTOS**
- **SOCIAL MEDIA MANAGER**

Manufactured by Amazon.ca
Bolton, ON

16196478R00105